... In the green spring

BLUE HAIKU

Lydia MONTIGNY

BLUE HAIKU

Mentions légales

© 2021 Lydia MONTIGNY

Éditeur : BoD-Books on Demand
12-14 rond-point des Champs-Élysées, 75008 Paris
Impression : Books on Demand, Norderstedt, Allemagne

ISBN : 978-2-3222-5063-9
Dépôt légal : Mai 2021

Livres précédents :

* Dans le Vent (VII 2017)
* Ecrits en Amont (VIII 2017)
* Jeux de Mots (VIII 2017)
* Etoile de la Passion (VIII 2017)
* As de Cœur (XI 2017)
* Pensées Eparses et Parsemées (XI 2017)
* Le Sablier d'Or (XI 2017)
* Rêveries ou Vérités (I 2018)
* Couleurs de l'Infini (II 2018)
* Exquis Salmigondis (V 2018)
* Lettres Simples de l'être simple (VI 2018)
* A l'encre d'Or sur la Nuit (X 2018)
* A la Mer, à la Vie (XI 2018)
* Le Cœur en filigrane (XII 2018)
* Le Silence des Mots (III 2019)
* La Musique Mot à Mot (IV 2019)
* Les 5 éléments (V 2019)
* Univers et Poésies (VIII 2019)
* Les Petits Mots (X 2019)
* Au Jardin des Couleurs (XI 2019)
* 2020 (XII 2019)
* Nous... Les Autres (X 2020)
* Ombre de soie (III 2020)
* Les Jeux de l'Art (IV 2020)
* Harmonie (VI 2020)
* La source de l'Amour (VIII 2020)
* Au pays des clowns (X 2020)
* 365 (XI 2020)
* L'Amour écrit... (XII 2020)
* Haïkus du Colibri (II 2021)
* Le Bonzaï d'Haïkus (IV 2021)

The Seine is flowing.

Under a lonely bridge

Hush! Paris by night

Lake of memories

Elegance of a swan

Reflection of a smile

Tenderness of Life

Between our two pas de deux

Dance the infinite

To write the impossible

To cheat the insomnia of the soul

Always hope

To listen to the sea

Its slight sway

Song of a shell

Moment of harmony

The snow gently blossoms

Music of hope

Day of Solitude

Without reflection in the mirror

To be or not to be

Fluttering flakes

The shores of the silent lake

A swan passes by

Harvest day

For the hungry blackbirds

Champagne cork

Upside down worms

Smiling at memories

The bat laughs

The rose of words

Blossoming in the four winds

Sun at its zenith

Sun at its zenith

Tightrope walker between two trees

Vertical Vertigo

Spring morning

In an exciting ballet

The nests are rounding

Every season

Passes in the one before

Life remembers

A spider weaves

Between two large catalpas

Indian dream catcher

Ocean of flowers

Respiration of the wind

The swallow is here

The wind in the bell

Chips the silence

Mantilla in the sky

A long carf of mist

Floating on the silver lake

The pink flamingo

Sweet spring song

In the midst of the almond trees

My ideas forage

To walk with bare feet

To gather flowers of silence

To listen to your heart

To take a break

On the forgotten path

To understand the time

Day of indulgence

In the reflect of the mirror

Mute imitation

Through the blind slats

White note on score

Musical moon

To walk in the night

Like a ghost, like a moon,

The forest hoots

Path under the steps

Of the secret of hope

The wise man is silent

Quiet force

That time does not stop

The elephant carries it

Sun is suspended

In the blue branches of the sky

Confetti of flowers

To think softly

In the power of silence

Love is right

To create by chance

A will of destiny

Birth of the Art

Spring snows

Pink flakes and white petals

Seasons get married

To mark a page

By a badly polished pebble

The wind is curious

A day of weakness

A thoughtful silence

After the siesta

Light in the evening

Ephemeral on a mirror

Reflected moment

An Indian summer

The tender breath of life

El condor pasa

Black and white Springtime

Art of mathematics

Nest of "3.14

Day of silence

Time passes slowly

Sound of a teardrop

A long snowy day

Around a big wood fire

Melting chocolate

Pearls of light

Corollas of daffodils

The sunrise forages

Orange and lemon

Horizon bending over

Provencal sun

Horizon from the top down

Wonderful fresco of love.

Horizontal tree

Time of idleness

The way of memory

Morse code melody

Lapping of the lake

Pink banks of the cherry trees

The blue dragonfly

Poetry of a day

Invisible music

Indecipherable

To offer a star

To paint the world in a smile

To melt in your eyes

Mysterious jungle

Voice in the green leaves

Little monkey jumps

White frothy foam

Perfumed blue lagoon

The soap bubbles

First light of spring

caterpillar measures a leaf

The fine green lace

Morning mist

Sliding through the fingers

Ray of sunlight

Moonlight -

A perfume of flowers knocks quietly

On the door

Inventing tomorrow

The eyes on the horizon

The hearts entwined

Wooden rattle

Bicycle on a bridge

The breath of air

Lake of memories

Elegance of a swan

Reflection of a smile

Confetti of words

Caress of a hurricane.

Wandering love

Little ladybird

Wakes up in the white morning

Four-leaf clover

The stones speak

Carving the history of the world

Through the instinct

And the wisdom of men

Sparkles of pyrite

Spring in the wind

Swirling butterflies

A chrysalis

Flocks of clouds

White water lily on the lake

The transhumance

To wake up in the rain

Smell of musical flowers

To lie down in peace

Day of tidying up

In the garden of thoughts

Chimerical herbarium

A shadow breathes

Empty calm of the spirit.

The rain of the sun

Strange clear night

Invisible presence

Lonely echo

Old weeping willow

Whispering of living water

The mill is turning

Eye to eye

The invisible of the world

Time disappears

A bell rings

Fledglings in a nest

The cat stands still

Invisible Love

The silence forgives

Secret of strength

To iron the leaves

With a spring breeze

A horse shoe

Snowmelt

Rocks are moving the torrent

Both feet in the water

Day of solitude-

The tears of silence

Ignore the echo

Harmony of the body

Delicacy of gesture

The heart as a star

Pure watercolour

Trouble in the secret garden

Cameos of Love

Seeds of Autumn

Becoming leaves in spring

Surprised squirrel

A moment of doubt

The heart makes no mistake

The blue rose

An art gallery

Signed by illustrious unknowns

Naturally

Sigh of a feather

Fluttering in the calm

Sweet quietude

Passion for Life

Crystalline and joyful

Smile of Love

Day of freedom

To breathe with a smile

The springtime of the air

Stopover in the Sky

A thousand stars in your eyes

Cuddly poetry

Birds in silence

Coming together on the branches :

Library

To paint simply

A single stroke, a single colour

The mind does the rest

To walk in the night

Of forests and great lakes

To believe in each step

To take a break

The music leaves a void-

The dance is slipping in

Haiku on a wall

Look at the unfinished

An eternity